My Cows

By Heather Miller

Children's Press
A Division of Grolier Publishing
New York / London / Hong Kong / Sydney
Danbury, Connecticut

Special thanks to the Koon family and for the use of their farm, Koon Jersey Farm

Photo Credits: Cover and all photos by Thaddeus Harden

Contributing Editor: Jennifer Ceaser
Book Design: MaryJane Wojciechowski

Visit Children's Press on the Internet at:
http://publishing.grolier.com

Cataloging-in-Publication Data

Miller, Heather.
   My cows / by Heather Miller.
     p. cm. — (My farm)
   Includes bibliographical references and index.
   Summary: A young boy explains how he cares for his
cows and defines the words "calf" and "dairy cow."
   ISBN 0-516-23106-5 (lib. bdg.) — ISBN 0-516-23031-X (pbk.)
   1. Dairy cattle—Juvenile literature. 2. Cows—
Juvenile literature. [1. Dairy cattle. 2. Cows]
   I. Title. II. Series.
   SF208.M56 2000   00-024386
   636.2'142 dc21

Contents

Hi, I'm Chase.

Welcome to my farm!

Would you like to meet my cows?

5

I have two cows.

My cows are **dairy cows**.

Dairy cows make milk.

Every day, Dad takes my brother and me to the **barn**.

We are going to milk the cows.

We bring **pails** to hold the milk.

Dad and I milk the cows.

We milk the cows until the pails are full.

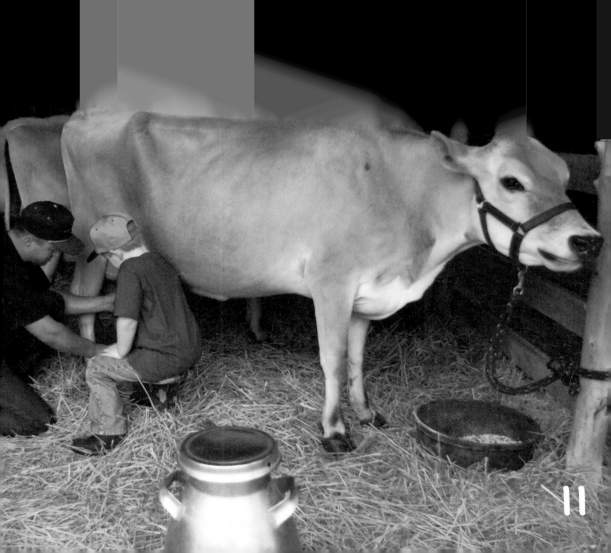

My cows give us milk.

One of my cows has another job.

Are you ready for a surprise?

13

Beauty is a mother cow.

She has a new **calf**.

A calf is a baby cow.

15

My cows eat grass in the **field**.

Eating grass is good for cows.

It makes their milk taste good.

17

I also give my cows **grain** to eat.

My brother gives them water to drink.

At the end of the day, my cows sleep in the barn.

It is clean and warm in the barn.

Goodnight, my cows!

21

New Words

barn (**barn**) a place where farm
   animals stay
calf (**kaf**) a baby cow
dairy cows (**dair**-ee **kowz**) cows
   that give milk
field (**feeld**) a piece of land
   covered with grass
grain (**grayn**) food that cows eat
pails (**paylz**) pots with handles
   used to carry things, such as milk

22

To Find Out More

Books

From Cow to Ice Cream
by Bertram T. Knight
Children's Press

Milk: From Cow to Carton
by Aliki
HarperCollins Juvenile Books

Raising Cows on the Koebels' Farm
by Alice K. Flanagan
Children's Press

Web Site

Barnyard Buddies
http://www.execpc.com/~byb/
Meet the Barnyard Buddies and learn more about farm animals. The site includes games and posters to color. Write an e-mail to your favorite animal!

Index

About the Author
Heather Miller lives in Cambridge, Massachusetts, with her son, Jasper. She is a graduate student at Harvard University.

Reading Consultants
Kris Flynn, Coordinator, Small School District Literacy, The San Diego County Office of Education

Shelly Forys, Certified Reading Recovery Specialist, W.J. Zahnow Elementary School, Waterloo, IL

Peggy McNamara, Professor, Bank Street College of Education, Reading and Literacy Program